Play Strategic Golf: Course Navigation

How To Position Yourself To Score Like The Pros

Eric Jones

2014 Northern California PGA Teacher of the Year
2-time World Long Drive Champion
Master's Degree in Sport Psychology
www.EricJonesGolf.com

Published by Birdie Press

This book is available in quantity at special discounts for your group or organization. For further information please contact:

Birdie Press
21 C Orinda Way #236
Orinda, CA 94563
www.birdiepress.com

Cover design by Brian Johnson

ISBN:0984417117
ISBN-13:9780984417117

CONTENTS

WHY PLAY STRATEGIC GOLF?

How would you like to take 6 to 10 shots off your score the next time you play?

Without changing your swing.

Without practicing.

Without doing anything fundamentally different except thinking differently and integrating a few strategic principles into your game?

I'm going to show you how you can improve your scores by changing the way you play the game, rather than by changing the way you swing. For the average golfer, that could be as many as 6 to 10 shots off your scores per round.

And it's not hard to do, once you know what you should be paying attention to on the course.

All you need is a framework and a series of practical guidelines that will help you understand how to think better and make better strategic decisions. This book, and the other books in the Play Strategic Golf series, will give you those guidelines and the framework. The Strategic Golf Framework©.

I've been playing golf for over 50 years, for most of them as a scratch or plus handicap. I played college golf at Stanford and after graduating served as the JV/Assistant coach. As an amateur I played a lot of tournament golf and had my share of success.

But it wasn't until 2003, when I won the World Long Drive Championship, turned Pro, and then went through the PGA Professional training program that I started to *study* golf. At the same time I went back to school to study Sport Psychology to learn the mental side of performance. The combination helped me understand what it took to consistently play my *best* golf. Before then I had just played. Any strategy I used on the course was picked up by listening to others or learning the hard way — by making lots of mistakes.

The main purpose of the Play Strategic Golf series is to share ideas and concepts about playing smarter golf. In particular concepts that have little, if anything, to do with the actual golf swing, yet have a huge impact on your score.

Too much of the information being fed to golfers by the popular media is about the mechanics of the golf swing. Swing mechanics is only one part of golf — the ball-striking part of game management. Mechanics is not the be-all and end-all answer to playing better.

Play Strategic Golf: Course Navigation brings together and consolidates fundamental concepts about *playing golf*, not golf swing. These are concepts that I wish someone had shared with me when I was learning the game. I would have been spared a lot of time and grief. This book, and the entire Play Strategic Golf series, will help you jump past many of the things it normally takes years of playing to learn.

Play Strategic Golf will help you cut through the clutter. There is so much information available on golf that it is very difficult to know what is really important when it comes to scoring. It is even more difficult to understand how it all fits together, especially when much of the information seems contradictory.

There is a large population of golfers who don't take lessons, who don't have the time to practice, or who simply aren't motivated to practice. Yet they still want to improve their scores. These golfers need and deserve help as well, without forcing them to choose to do something they don't want to do and don't necessarily enjoy.

Over the years I've evolved my teaching practice to include elements of scoring, shot-making, and mental skills alongside the traditional swing mechanics instruction most golfers expect. But I seldom have the opportunity within the constraints of a 1-hour lesson to spend the kind of time needed to share insights on how to *play* better golf and what it takes to *score*. That's where this book comes in.

The information in this book is based on years of study. It's based on years of practical application to my own game. It's based on conversations and insights from some of the best golfers in the world — PGA Tour professionals. And it's based on practical experience gained from thousands of playing lessons with students of all abilities, helping them shave strokes from their scores in the only place it really matters — on the golf course.

There *IS* a way to improve your scores without spending countless hours on the range and without feeling like you have to have a perfect golf swing. That's what this book is about: sharpening your mental edge so you can play a smarter game.

If you'd like help beyond the Play Strategic Golf books there is a Resources page at the end of this book. You should also consider my monthly online coaching program at Performance Coaching which you can find at www.EricJonesGolf.com.

In the meantime, enjoy this book and use the ideas to start playing your best golf and shooting your lowest scores.

Let's tee it up!

•

A FRAMEWORK FOR BETTER GOLF

There are three books that make up the Play Strategic Golf series: Course Navigation, Game Management, and Mental Toughness (the essential skill of Self Management). Together these three books address the three key facets of the game that determine your performance every time you play.

The Play Strategic Golf series will provide you with organizing principles, guidelines, and rules-of-thumb you can use on the course to play better, smarter golf. Understanding how to successfully manage and improve your performance in these three key game areas will improve your ability to play. Putting these guidelines into action is how you will consistently play your best golf.

The principles that follow are meant to be actionable. They are organized to fit the way you play and the way you need to think in the course.

Most students I speak with want to play better on the course, but don't have a simple system to accomplish their goal. They come to me for lessons, thinking the answer must be in better mechanics or fixing their swing problems. What they really want is to improve their scores and their enjoyment of the game.

A strategic framework is the answer.

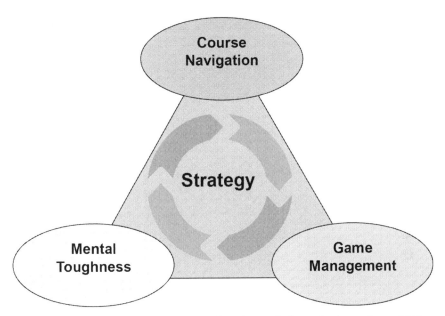

What you'll take away from this book, and the whole series of Play Strategic Golf books, is a framework that shows you how course navigation, game management, and self management all work together to help you create your strategy decisions so you can play smarter golf.

With the right framework, you'll know what factors you need to consider when devising your strategy for the golf course, for each hole, and for each shot.

Understanding what factors go into each strategy decision will help you start making smarter navigational decisions about where you want to position your ball on each shot. You'll make better game management choices about which club will get the job done. Picking the right strategy for the right reasons will allow you to play with more aggressiveness, confidence and mental toughness. More confidence will improve your swing and your scores. Plus you'll have more fun when you play!

The Benefit of a Framework for Managing Your Game

The beauty of having a framework is that it allows you to compartmentalize information and actions so they are easier to understand and manage. Frameworks are nothing more than ways to organize information or actions into separate, smaller units that show how the parts relate to each other and to the whole.

Think of the three game facets as three separate buckets.

Everything you do on the golf course will fit into one of these three buckets. The buckets facilitate your strategy decisions for each shot. To develop a solid strategy for a shot or a hole you simply make sure you have considered factors arising from each of the three buckets.

The buckets are like having a checklist. When it's time to develop a strategy for your next shot you check off all the factors in bucket one, then bucket two, and then bucket three. If you get a green light from each bucket, you are ready to make your shot. If not, you continue cycling back and forth between the buckets until you arrive at a green light strategy.

The Strategic Golf Framework Makes it Simple

The process for checking off your bucket list boils down to three simple questions you ask yourself before each shot:

1. **What does this shot require? (course navigation)**
2. **Do I have that shot? (game management)**
3. **Can I commit to the shot? (self management)**

Three Keys To Scoring Questions

Having a consistent process to go through for each situation actually speeds up your decision-making:

- You aren't distracted by unnecessary factors;
- You aren't sitting around trying to figure out what you are supposed to be figuring out;
- You make better decisions more quickly;
- You have more confidence in your plan of action; and
- You will be able to totally commit to your shot.

When you know your strategy is sound you can relax and focus fully on making your shot. Tension creeps in whenever there is lingering doubt or indecision. Tension kills your swing speed and your consistency. Confident, tension-free swings are more reliable and produce better results.

The Problem with Unconscious Decision-Making

You probably already consider factors from the buckets to form your hole-by-hole and shot-by-shot strategy. But it is more than likely an unconscious process. And it has been my experience, based on the thousands of playing lessons I've conducted over the years, that you probably don't routinely check the factors from *all three buckets* before forming your strategy.

My observation is that over time golfers gain a vast amount of experience in a variety of different situations with different shots, different clubs, and different yardages, all under different conditions. That experience tends to get lumped into a very large bucket, full of both good experiences and not-so-good experiences.

Out of this large bucket of experience the golfer tries to craft generalizations. These generalizations help them create and select a strategy for the current shot.

Sometimes the strategies work, sometimes they don't.

Whenever a shot doesn't work the strategy tends to get filed against the general guideline in the "that doesn't work very well" category. Over time, the "that doesn't work very well" experiences pile up. Without a framework these negative experiences fill a very large bucket which can dramatically erode your confidence. The decision making process is clouded by the unconscious weight of all those past negative results.

Having a framework, on the other hand, makes it far easier to categorize your game. It makes it easier to analyze your play and understand where you need to focus your improvement efforts.

If you have a tough day on the course and you have no framework, you might be tempted to think your whole game is off.

With a framework you can narrow the primary issue to one bucket, and maybe even pinpoint it to one particular aspect within that bucket. When that's the case, you know exactly where to focus your attention during practice in order to improve, and you won't waste your time trying to fix things that aren't really broken. Your decisions will become more of a conscious process.

Pay Deliberate Attention

Playing better golf and shooting lower scores is about paying deliberate attention to each key game area, on every hole and on every shot.

Course Navigation will show you how to make your strategic decisions a conscious process. Consciously paying deliberate attention will enable you to develop and refine your strategic decision-making process so that you can constantly improve the way you play.

Course Navigation is organized into a number of principles to use while playing. I've kept this book short and to-the-point, so you can easily use the ideas right away when you play. An overly complex book or a book that is too long to read won't help you.

As you read about each of the principles, you will want to generalize them to situations you have faced on the course.

After you read each course navigation principle, give yourself time to think about how you would apply that particular principle in a variety of different situations. Think about how you have applied similar principles in the past. The more scenarios you can recall from past rounds where you made the right decision — and where you *didn't* make the right decision — the easier it will be for you to recall the principle the next time you play and put it to good use.

In the next chapter we'll get an overview of course navigation, and I'll explain why I refer to it as course navigation rather than course management.

•

WHY CALL IT COURSE NAVIGATION?

Why do I call it "course navigation" instead of "course management"?

"Course Management" is the term most familiar to golfers. Everybody knows you need to practice good course management in order to score well. If I suggest to a student before a round that they need to practice good course management they'd nod and say "Yes. Practice good course management. Good idea. I'll do it."

But when I ask students to *define* course management suddenly the concept starts to get elusive.

What is Course Management?

How would you define course management?

Could you rattle off the main principles behind course management?

Would you be able to explain what "good course management" actually means when you are on the golf course?

What are the practical applications of good course management?

If you falter when you try to provide specific answers to these questions, you are not alone.

COURSE MANAGEMENT
is really
COURSE NAVIGATION

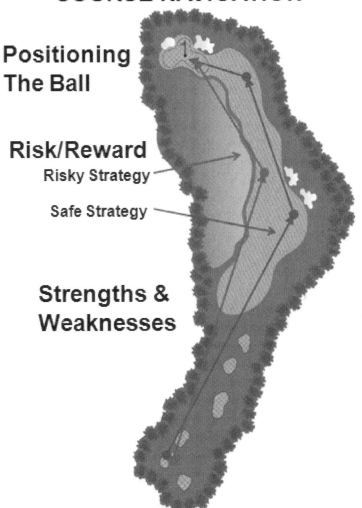

**Positioning
The Ball**

Risk/Reward

Risky Strategy

Safe Strategy

**Strengths &
Weaknesses**

There seems to be an underlying assumption that golfers already understand what course management means and that they know how to put it into practice when playing. Nothing could be farther from the truth.

In our golf culture we talk about good course management and we agree that good course management is crucial, but we seldom discuss how to *execute* good course management.

It's far easier to talk about executing mechanical swing motions — like a good weight shift or a proper swing plane — than it is to talk about course management. Swing mechanics are things you can see and measure and do. Because it's easier to talk about things we can see and do, we tend to fall into the trap of focusing on just that part of the game. That's the fallacy of always looking at swing mechanics for an answer. It's easier.

But it's not always the right answer.

The challenge with talking about course management coherently is that every situation and circumstance is unique. That uniqueness is one reason why so little has been written about course management.

For example, a 90-yard approach shot may sound straightforward. But in truth the shot is unique — every time, for every player, and for every situation.

The course situations of lie, angles to the pin, weather, obstacles and hazards, etc., are never the same, even though we are referring to a 90-yard shot. Every player's skill level and shot-making capabilities are also different. Even the psychological circumstances are different: a 90-yard approach shot in the middle of a friendly round is vastly different from the same shot on the last hole of a major tournament when you need to hit it close to win.

It's hard to talk concretely about course management because there are so many variables. That's why you are better off with an understanding of general principles which you can then apply to specific situations on the course. The chapters that follow will provide you with the principles.

Course Management should be Course Navigation

The other reason I use "course navigation" is that I think the term "management" is vague when applied to a golf course. The vagueness is part of the problem when trying to get a handle on what course management means and how we are supposed to use it when we play.

The truth is you can't "manage" a course.

The golf course is what it is. There is nothing you can do to "manage" the course because you can't change the course. Whatever you face when you play is what you face. Since you can't change the golf course you can't manage it.

So what can you manage?

The answer is your strategy.

The one thing you can manage during the round is the way that you make decisions regarding where you want to hit your ball as you navigate your way from tee to green.

And since making your way from a starting point to an end point is really the art of "navigation," I refer to the process as course "navigation" rather than course "management."

Good course "navigation" entails getting safely around the golf course to minimize risk and maximize results by making the next shot as easy as possible. *Effective* course navigation means knowing where each shot on the hole needs to be, beginning with your putt on the green and working backwards to the tee.

Thinking in terms of "navigation" rather than "management" will open new ways for you to look at each hole and each shot.

How Do We Implement Good Course Navigation?

Mark Twain wrote stories about riverboat pilots on the Mississippi. He himself was a riverboat pilot. Because the river was always changing the pilots helped each other by exchanging information about the location of new snags and sandbars. Armed with the latest information, the pilot could then navigate his boat to a position in the river to avoid the dangers *well in advance* of encountering the hazard. By positioning his boat on the safe side of the river in advance, the pilot could steam right past the hazards and ensure a safe journey.

So it is with golf course navigation.

It's all about positioning yourself to avoid hazards and having the straightest, most trouble-free shot to your target.

The best way to arm you with the tools needed for good course navigation is to provide you with principles, or rules of thumb, to help you make better decisions as you play. Thus, the remainder of this book is organized into a series of practical course navigation principles that you can put to immediate use the next time you play.

So let's get started with Course Navigation Principle #1: Make the Next Shot Easier.

•

COURSE NAVIGATION PRINCIPLE #1
PLAN YOUR CURRENT SHOT
TO MAKE YOUR NEXT SHOT
AS EASY AS POSSIBLE

Your overriding course navigation principle should be to *always* plan your current shot so that your *next* shot is as easy as possible.

What this means is that Step One of your strategy for your current shot actually starts with the next shot. All that's required is a little thinking ahead.

There's usually some give and take between the current circumstances, your shot-making skills, and the risk/reward tradeoffs, which are described in more detail in the companion book *Play Strategic Golf: Game Management*. But the first step in figuring out what to do on your current shot is to determine what would make the next shot as easy as possible and then working backwards from there for each shot.

By zooming in on each shot we can see how a little advance planning can make the next shot easier, starting from the green and working backwards to the tee.

EXAMPLE #1: The graphic shows the entire process from the hole backwards to the tee. The easiest putt you could have is a straight, uphill putt. Start there.

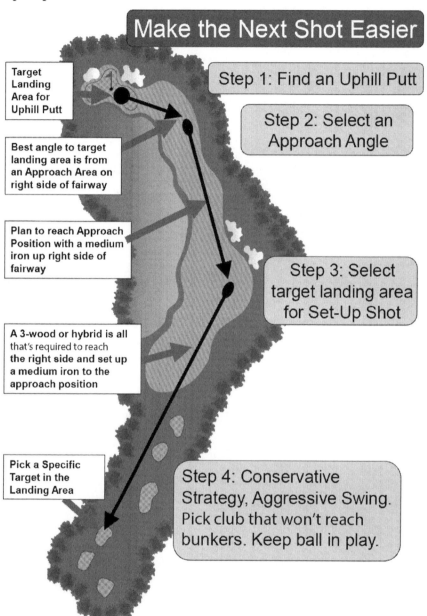

Make the Next Shot Easier

Target Landing Area for Uphill Putt

Step 1: Find an Uphill Putt

Best angle to target landing area is from an Approach Area on right side of fairway

Step 2: Select an Approach Angle

Plan to reach Approach Position with a medium iron up right side of fairway

Step 3: Select target landing area for Set-Up Shot

A 3-wood or hybrid is all that's required to reach the right side and set up a medium iron to the approach position

Pick a Specific Target in the Landing Area

Step 4: Conservative Strategy, Aggressive Swing. Pick club that won't reach bunkers. Keep ball in play.

In order to have an easy uphill putt we need to understand the slope of the green around the pin. Identifying the area of the green below the hole provides us with the target landing area.

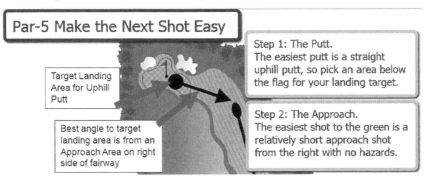

Once we know the target landing area on the green we can look backward to the fairway to determine a ball position that would provide the easiest approach shot that would give us the best chance of reaching the landing spot on the green and the avoid hazards.

In this example the easiest approach shot is a short wedge from the right side of the fairway. Coming in from the right allows us to avoid the water on the left and the bunker on the right.

Next we determine the best way to get our ball into the ideal approach wedge position. We need to think about the set-up shot.

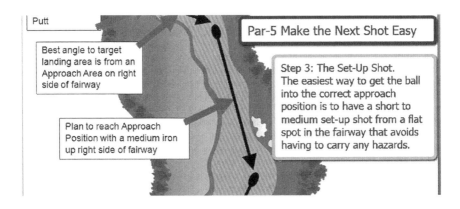

Looking back down the fairway from the approach position we see a corridor that avoids having to carry either the water or the fairway bunker for our set-up shot. The corridor points us to a position in the middle of the fairway that provides a medium iron shot from a flat lie.

Knowing where the ball should end up for our set-up shot tells us how we can make the tee shot easier. We want the ball to end up in the middle of the widest part of the fairway, short of the bunkers and safely away from the water. That allows us to pick a club for the tees shot that is more reliable and accurate than a driver, such as a 3-wood or hybrid. We tee up on the same side as the water so we can hit away from it, and since we know we can't reach the bunkers with less club, we can swing freely and aggressively.

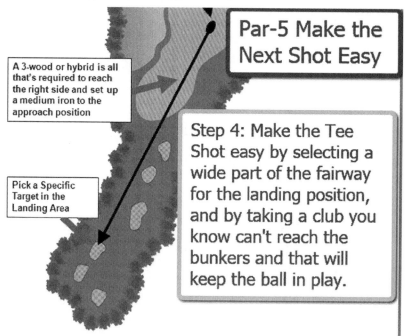

Par-5 Make the Next Shot Easy

A 3-wood or hybrid is all that's required to reach the right side and set up a medium iron to the approach position

Pick a Specific Target in the Landing Area

Step 4: Make the Tee Shot easy by selecting a wide part of the fairway for the landing position, and by taking a club you know can't reach the bunkers and that will keep the ball in play.

Like the river pilot, the question you should be asking is how to position yourself on the course so you can steer right past the hazards and ensure the most straightforward shot at your target.

Golf is a "positional" game. Playing for position rather than distance is the right strategy almost every time, particularly off the tee. Position yourself to make the next shot easier.

EXAMPLE #2: If you have the choice between taking driver off the tee which would result in a downhill lie on the next shot, vs. taking a 3-wood which would put you on a flat lie, the better strategic choice would be to take the 3-wood. Even though you might give up 20 yards with your 3-wood you'll hit the green more often from the flat lie. It's an easier shot from a flat lie. That's how you think about making the next shot easier.

EXAMPLE #3: Let's use a sharp dog-leg for another example.

It's tempting to always think in terms of cutting the corner on a dogleg to make the next shot shorter into the green. Shorter is better, right? But it's not always the wisest navigation strategy. You have to know what your next shot will look like to know if you are making the shot easier.

Take a look at the graphic. It's a dogleg right with bunkers and trees guarding the right side of the fairway.

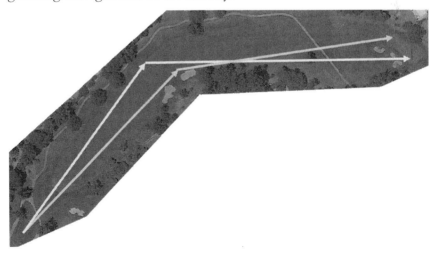

What would happen if you tried to cut the corner on this hole?

It depends on where the pin is located.

This is an example of a real hole. The graphic is taken from one of my other books: *"How To Make A Yardage Book"* (on Amazon). Cutting the corner will give you a much shorter second shot to the green. Playing to the left side of the fairway will avoid the hazards (the fairway bunkers and the trees on the left) at the expense of having an approach shot that is several clubs longer.

In this example the critical decision point about what will make the 2nd shot easier is the pin location.

If the pin is in the front left (red pin) then cutting the corner may be a reasonable risk because you'd have a straight shot at the pin. There are no hazards in the way on the second shot. That is an easier shot, with a shorter club.

You'd have to balance that off against your skill at hitting fairway bunker shots because cutting the corner brings the bunkers into play. Is the trade-off of picking up 10 extra yards and hitting one club less worth the downside of possibly hitting from a fairway bunker? That's actually a game management question, but it does influence your course navigation options and decisions.

If it is a blue pin in the back right, however, then the trees will be in the way for the second shot even if you do cut the corner. Having to slice a shot around the trees into a back pin guarded by bunkers in front of the green is a very difficult shot. Plus you'd bring the fairway bunkers into play on your drive.

In this case it is far better to play to the left side of the fairway in order to have an easier, straight shot at the back right pin. You might have to take two or three clubs more to reach the green. But it is still an easier shot. Statistically, over time, you will shoot lower scores taking a more conservative approach.

It's all about making the next shot easier.

EXAMPLE #4: This is one of my favorites. It comes up regularly during playing lessons on long par-4s when the golfer can't reach the green (or maybe could, but it would have to be a perfectly-hit shot).

The question is this: do you go for the green, or do you lay back and have a longer shot in?

The answer is ... it depends.

It depends on the hazards surrounding the green, how far you hit your 3-wood or hybrid, and your "no-man's land" yardage. Here's how we determine the answer.

1. *Keep the ball in play.* If there are bunkers, water, OB, or other hazards around the green, make the choice to keep the ball in play. Laying up should be your first choice. You can still make par with a great chip or putt. But you run the risk of shooting big numbers when you bring hazards into play. Hitting from a hazard is not an easier next shot.

2. *Conservative Strategy, Aggressive Swing.* If you choose the navigation strategy to lay up and keep your ball short of the hazards, take a club you *absolutely know* will not reach the hazard. Then make an aggressive swing. Don't try to ease up on your 3-wood or hybrid. Pick the spot in the fairway that will give you the easiest line to the flag and make an aggressive swing with a shorter club to get to that spot.

3. *Stay away from your "No-Man's-Land" Yardage.* Every golfer has a yardage range from the green that would result in a half-swing or less. For the male average golfer the range is usually between 35 to 70 yards. Anything less than a half-swing requires great touch, which can only be developed through practice. With less than a half-swing it is very difficult to control the swing, trajectory and spin. The less-than-half-swing is a very difficult shot, even for PGA Tour pros.

Strategy to Avoid "No-Man's Land" Yardages

When your lay-up navigation choices could result in your ball ending up in your no-man's land, the strategy I recommend to students is as follows: If you can safely get the ball within 35 yards or less of the green and stay out of hazards or trouble, go for it. If the club you want to hit would put you in no-man's land, take less club and lay up to a position that will give you a 3/4 or full swing.

Research shows that the closer your proximity to the hole the better your odds of getting up and down ... unless it means your ball will end up in no-man's land.

If the lay-up shot would result in your ball ending up in no-man's land then the answer is to lay back to have a full-swing or 3/4-swing. Get yourself to somewhere between 70 to 100 yards from the green. This will allow you to control the distance, trajectory and spin. Plus it results in a fuller, more comfortable swing that is much more reliable in the long run.

Learning how to get your ball close to the flag on 70-yard to 125-yard shots is one of the five most important shots in golf. They are called Scoring Shots for a reason. Developing the skill to get the ball close with your wedges will give you the confidence to lay back when faced with one of these no-man's land decisions.

The shot is so important that I developed a video-based training program around it — one that I've used since the days I was coaching at Stanford. Pick up a copy of *"Scoring Clubs"* at www.EricJonesGolf.com and learn how to dial in your yardages on these critical approach shots.

Note: This example includes making a specific club choice to either reach the green in two or lay up. The decision about club and shot choice actually falls within the category of game management rather than course navigation. But since the shot selection also has to factor in the spot where you want your ball to end up there is still an element of course navigation involved in your decision.

The point is that even though this book is focused on course navigation, the golfer's skill level, physical ability, and commitment to the shot always contribute to the final shot as well as the club selection decision.

This scenario is one of my favorites because when it comes up during a playing lesson the student nearly always makes the wrong initial club choice and decides to go for the green. That gives me an excellent opportunity to provide some coaching, which I do by having them play two balls.

Golfers think that because it is a par-4, they should be getting home in two. So they automatically pull the longer club, regardless of the hazards near the green or pin placement. The results are predictably disastrous, so I make sure to carry an extra ball in my pocket.

When their first ball inevitably finds the hazard I coach them through a different strategy.

I give them a club that will put them either inside 35 yards or at 75 yards, depending on what is around the green and the hole location. Then I coach them to select a landing spot on the fairway that will give them a clear path to the pin with lots of green to work with. They play each ball out, keeping score.

From experience I can tell you that golfers make par more often with the conservative strategy than by trying to hit a long club. That alone should make it a strategy worth adopting. But the real benefit is that with the conservative strategy they avoid big numbers, because they avoid bringing a double-bogey or worse into play.

The key lesson is that you are always thinking backwards from the next shot to the current shot to make the next shot as easy as possible. Hitting from a hazard is not an easy shot.

This kind of backwards thinking makes for good forward planning (*there's* a mind-bending sentence!). But if you carry the thought process out to its logical conclusion you'll immediately realize that planning the next shot also provides a clear road map for planning your strategy to play the entire hole.

This leads us to Course Navigation Principle #2: Play the Hole Backwards.

•

COURSE NAVIGATION PRINCIPLE #2
PLAN YOUR STRATEGY FOR EACH HOLE FROM THE CUP BACK TO THE TEE

In order to figure out how to make your next shot easier you actually have to think ahead to the next shot, which means you have to think ahead to the next shot, and then the next shot after that until you finally hole out.

What that really means is that you create your strategy from the cup back to the tee shot.

And this is fun because now we can get practical and see how good course navigation really works.

How Course Navigation Really Works

If we start from the cup and work backwards, we start our strategic planning with putting.

The easiest putt we can have is a straight, uphill putt.

So we create a navigation plan that will put us on the green in a spot below the hole with a straight uphill putt. *All you have to know is which way the green slopes and where the pin is.* That will tell us where the landing area should be.

Take a moment on the tee box before each hole to think about the pin placement and the easiest way to reach it. That will tell you how to play your approach shot and your tee shot.

Note: When possible get a pin sheet showing the daily pin placements. If a pin sheet is not available, look at the greens on the holes in front of you or to the side as you play to note the pin locations as you see them. For example, if you can see the 9th green while you are standing on the 1st tee (which is fairly common), make a note of the pin location so you know the pin location before playing the hole. Knowing where the pins are will give you an edge when you create your strategy for the hole later in the round.

A second way you can get hole-by-hole information is by visiting the golf course website. Often the course will have detailed hole-by-hole screen shots or playing advice, accompanied by graphics. Print them out and make your own yardage book. It will serve you well when you play.

If you don't have a pin sheet and the course does not supply hole-specific graphics or information, there are all kinds of Apps and GPS devices that can give you detailed information about the course and each hole. You can even go to Google Earth to see a 3-D image of each hole (which is what I recommend you use in my book "*How To Make A Yardage Book*").

Use the tools. But use them in a way that is much smarter than the way most golfers use them — by looking at the entire hole and working backwards to create your strategy.

If you still don't have any Apps or GPS devices that show you hole details, here are a few guidelines that will help you make an educated guess about where you want your ball to end up on the green.

Determine Slope of the Green

If you've never played the course before and you can't even see the green from the tee, figuring out the slope and pin placement can be a little tough. But we can make some educated guesses based on general golf course design rules and terrain characteristics, and develop a strategy from there.

Most greens slope from back to front. That's a common design feature because greens have to have at least 1^0 degree of slope for water drainage. Greens are also normally tilted toward the fairway approach corridor because it helps with depth perception.

Here are a couple more general slope tendencies: If there are mountains nearby the greens will tend to slope away from the mountains. If there is water most greens will tend to slope toward the water.

Ok. That information will give us the general tendencies for the slope of most greens. It's not as good as actually knowing the slope of the green — which is what you should be mapping during a practice round, and it doesn't necessarily take into account tiers and undulations. (For more information on mapping greens get a copy of *"How To Make A Yardage Book"* on Amazon).

But it's a start. We can at least make an educated guess. And we can start planning our navigation strategy and shot placement positions for the hole from the tee.

Determine Pin Placement

Next we figure out where the pin is.

Here are a few more facts about what to expect on the green for pin placements.

Most golf courses employ a 3-position pin rotation: front, middle, and back. Normally the pin position is indicated by the color of the flag: red for front, white for middle, and blue for back.

If the first green has a front pin, the second will have a middle pin and the third a back pin. The fourth hole starts the rotation all over with a front pin position. If you know one or two pin placements, you'll usually know where the rest will be for the remainder of the holes.

The next day when the cups are moved the front pin will be moved to the middle, the middle pin to the back, and the back pin will come around to the front, and so forth. Rotating pin positions keeps the green from getting worn out.

In addition, when architects design greens they not only think in terms of front, middle and back; they also think in terms of left side and right side. That gives them six possible pin locations, which allows for a variety of different breaks and slopes as well as different approach shots and angles.

On an 18-hole course you will usually find one third of the pins are in the front, one third in the middle, and one third in the back, usually in rotation.

Another factor to keep in mind is that in addition to front/middle/back pin placements there are also usually six "easy", six "medium", and six hard or "sucker" pin placements.

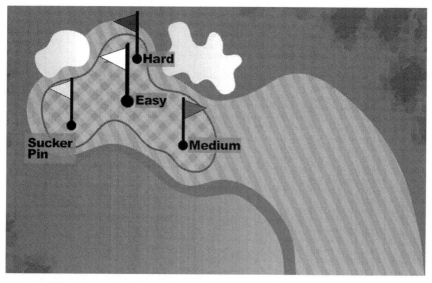

Quite often the back pins are the most difficult pins while the middle pins are generally the most accessible.

Armed with the knowledge of pin locations we can move on to the next rule of thumb to decide which pins to go for and which pin placements dictate a shot to a safe portion of the green. That's what we mean by recommending you take a few minutes before teeing off to determine your strategy for that hole. With some pin placements the only way you'll be able to get your approach shot close to the hole will be to position your ball on one side of the fairway.

•

COURSE NAVIGATION PRINCIPLE #3
ONLY ATTACK EASY PINS

As a rule of thumb, aim directly at the easy pins, and play to the middle of the green or a safe area on the green when facing the medium, hard and sucker pin placements.

Sucker pins get their name for a reason — they are usually tucked behind a hazard. Don't get suckered into going straight at these pin placements and risk big numbers unless you happen to have a straight shot at the pin where the hazard does not come into play. Think about making a great putt from an approachable position on the green rather than an exceptional approach shot.

These are generalizations, of course, but having this knowledge can help you determine when to take risks and when to play safe.

Ever hear the Pros talk about "being patient?"

Guess what they are referring to? The easy pin placements. They patiently wait for holes and shots where they can play to their strengths and then take dead aim at the flag.

For tough or sucker pins they play to the middle of the green and take trouble out of play.

Step 1: Find Your Landing Quadrant on the Green

Once you have an idea of where the pin is the next step is to figure out where to hit your approach shot. One of the easiest ways to do this is to divide the green into quadrants with the pin in the middle of the axis.

Remember, the strategic goal is to hit your approach shot to a spot below the hole so you have an uphill putt.

Figure out which quadrant is the downslope quadrant, and that becomes your target landing area.

In the illustration there are arrows on the green to indicate the slope of the green. The direction of the arrows provides the direction of the slope. The size of the arrows indicates the severity of the slope: longer arrows for a more severe slope and shorter arrows for a milder slope. This is the way we typically see green complexes marked on yardage books.

We've divided the green into quadrants with the axis through the pin. That makes it possible to determine the best landing area for an uphill putt, which is in the lower right quadrant as shown by the shaded area.

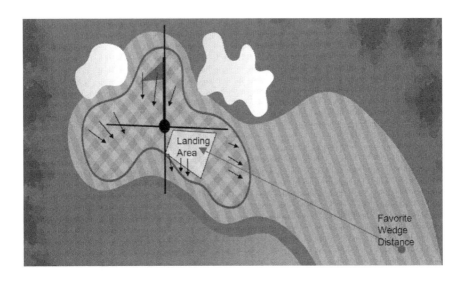

In my book *"How to Make A Yardage Book"* you'll find more specific details on how to mark your yardage book during practice rounds to determine the slopes and landing areas on the green. The process of creating a yardage book will cause you to really look at the green, which in turn will help you make better strategic decisions.

Step 2: Find an Approach Angle with the Easiest Path to Your Landing Area

Once you have divided the green into quadrants and identified your landing area the next step is to decide which spots on the fairway will give you the best and safest approach line to the landing area.

You'll notice in the graphic that there is an arrow drawn from the fairway to the landing area indicating the approach shot. That spot in the fairway represents your favorite wedge distance, which is the approach distance from which you are the most accurate, most comfortable, and most consistent.

Good course navigation dictates that you hit your ball to a spot on the fairway that will give you a straight shot at the landing area without having to go over hazards. If the pin was in the back left corner of the green you might have to hit your set-up shot farther down the fairway into the right corner to avoid having to carry the water on your approach to the pin.

Do you have challenges getting your approach wedge shots close to the pin? You are not alone. Studies show that the average 90s golfer only hits the green about 50% of the time from 100 yards. Contrast that to the Tour Pros who are disappointed if they are not within 15 feet of the pin from scoring wedge distance.

If you'd like some help with your scoring wedges I put together a few training videos that can help you. They are part of the Scoring Clubs training program. Click the link under the Resources page on my site at www.EricJonesGolf.com to watch free scoring shots training videos on how to hit these critical shots.

With these two simple examples it's easy to understand why it is so important to start the planning process from the hole and then work backwards. It's all about setting up the next shot.

Let's see how it works for the entire hole.

How to Plan Your Strategy from the Cup to the Tee

Now let's look at the entire hole and see how we'd create a strategy to play the hole from the cup backwards.

For this example we'll use a par-5 to show the navigation decision points on multiple shots. Note, however, that this same decision making process will also apply to a long par-4 for golfers who know they cannot reach the green in two shots.

We already know from our earlier example that the pin is in the middle of the green and that the landing area is in the lower right quadrant – the front left part of the green. Because this is a par-5, we have to decide whether to play it as a 3-shot hole or go for the green in two.

I discuss how to make that decision in the companion book *Play Strategic Golf: Game Management* and risk/reward as it applies to your shot-making and ball-striking skill level.

For now, though, we'll consider risk/reward from a golf course design viewpoint.

Understanding Risk/Reward

A well-designed golf hole will have an element of risk/reward. If you are willing to take the risk and you pull off the shot, you'll be rewarded with a lower score or a closer approach shot. If you don't pull off the shot, however, you'll pay a much higher price for taking the gamble.

RISK/REWARD

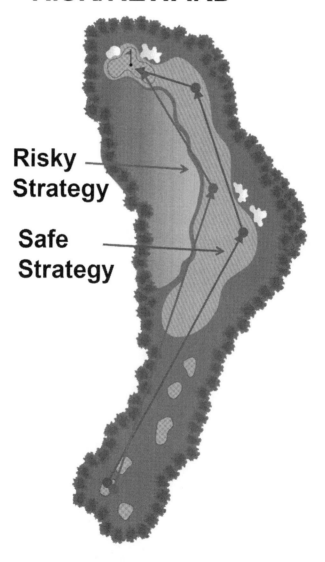

Risky Strategy

Safe Strategy

It's your job to figure out what the course architect had in mind when they designed the hole.

For instance, most greens are guarded by some sort of hazard or obstacle like bunkers, water, mounds, depressions, rough, or trees. These hazardous obstacles are used strategically by the golf course architect to add the element of risk/reward and to force you to make decisions on each shot.

The hazards are usually on either the right or left hand side of the green (sometimes both sides), and most often come into play when a golfer chooses an aggressive line or angle to the pin.

What that means, however, is the architect also usually leaves one side of the green (or the middle) "open", or free of hazards along the line of flight.

When that's the case we say the green "opens up" from the left, right, or center, so that there is always a "safe" way to play the hole.

That means there are usually at least two ways to play any hole: aggressively or conservatively. But this decision has to take into account the pin placement, your ability to position your approach shot, and your shot-making skill level.

How do you decide when to play conservatively or aggressively?

Play aggressively ONLY when the rewards are worth the risk and fall within your ball-striking skill level.

Let's say, for example, that the hole you are playing has a "sucker" pin placement tucked close to the edge of the green and surrounded by hazards. When you are standing on the tee developing your navigation strategy you already know that you won't be shooting directly at the pin. You'll be shooting at the middle of the green because there are no spots in the fairway that provide a safe angle to the pin that fits within your ball-striking skill level.

In this case it makes no sense to take an aggressive line off the tee. There is no reward. Or, at least, the potential reward is not sufficient for the risk involved. Be patient. Plan a strategy that makes your shots as easy as possible (Principle #1). Play for par and move on to the next hole.

These are fairly common golf course design elements:

1. The aggressive line is rewarded by the payoff of potentially lower scores, but the trade off is dealing with the hazards.
2. The conservative line is rewarded by safer shots but the trade-off is usually longer approach shots.

Remember that your decisions should always be tempered by what the hole will give you (or not give you), your shot-making skill level, and your ability to commit to your strategy.

Imagine for a moment that the hole we've been using as an example is a long par-4 rather than a par-5. Far too often I've watched golfers of average ability pull out their driver and go for the risky strategy. Their usual rationale is "But driver is the only way I'll be able to reach the green in two." My response is "Yes, but it is not the only way to make par."

Let's take a deeper look at how to determine what the hole will and will not give you and how it influences your navigation decisions.

•

HOW TO UNDERSTAND A GOLF HOLE

Balancing risk/reward is one of the strategic choices you'll always be making on any given shot or hole. The goal in pointing this out is to give you advanced knowledge of the types of design elements the architect may bring into play to force you to consider the potential hazards or other challenges built into the hole. Let's take a moment to understand how golf holes are designed and the elements you can expect to see. It will help you play smarter golf.

We start by identifying strengths and weaknesses.

Identifying Hole Strengths and Weaknesses

When the architect includes a difficult element in the hole we call that a "strength" or "defense" of the hole. Hazards, doglegs, mounds, depressions, fairway slope, trees and even wind direction are all potential "strengths" of a hole, and they are the ways the architect defends against your attack.

The flip side is soft areas or weaknesses of a hole. Wide landing areas in the fairway, flat stretches of terrain, bail-out areas, flat parts of the green, approach angles with no hazards or obstacles in the line of flight, etc., are all examples of the "soft" elements of the hole. These are the areas from which you should be planning your attack.

When we conduct playing lessons with students this is one of the first things we teach them to see: strengths and weaknesses of the hole.

Like a chess match, it is your job to attack the hole, while it is the architect's job to defend the hole against your attack. The strengths of the hole are the defenses put in place by the architect to foil your attack. Understanding how the defenses are set up will help you plan a better attack.

Most amateurs don't think in terms of attack and defense. But better players do. That way they are not surprised by what they find on the course. The way to fast track your way to a better golf game is to start thinking like the better players. The best way to do that is to put yourself in the shoes of the other guy — the course architect.

Understanding the Natural Flow of a Golf Hole

Look at the hole from the designer's perspective the next time you are standing on the tee. Try to imagine what they must have seen before they carved the course out of the terrain.

Architects typically design holes with a centerline from the tee to a turning point, then from the turning point to the hole. Take a few moments to find the centerline. Then see if you can locate the turning point. The centerline and turning point marks the path and the natural flow of the hole.

Rather than fight the natural path of the hole, plan a navigation route that works off the centerline. You'll begin to see how the architect intended you to play the hole, and what natural defenses were put in place to protect against your attack.

- How does the slope of the fairway funnel shots away from or toward the centerline?
- How and where does the fairway narrow?
- What natural elements influence the tee shot?
- What hazard complexes and obstacles are used to pinch the fairway? The narrow areas are the natural defenses, often further protected by bunkers, trees, water, mounds, or rough.
- How does the fairway widen? The wide areas are the intended landing areas.

- What natural elements make up the green complex or protect it?
- What elements would the architect have added, particularly around the green, and why were they added in that particular location and configuration?

Once you have a feel for the natural path of the hole you'll want to take note of the fairway contours to see how they may help, or how they may require a certain shot. Concave fairways are friendly because they will feed the ball to the middle. Convex fairways are unfriendly because they feed the ball away from the fairway.

Likewise the slope of the fairway may serve either to help or as a natural defense. Work off the centerline of the hole to see how you can use the slope to your advantage, or guard against a bounce that will land you in trouble.

Work off the turning point to see how the architect intended you to approach the hole.

Strategic, Penal, and Heroic Holes

It's also important to ask what kind of hole you are playing: strategic, penal, or heroic?

Generally speaking strategic holes put a heavy emphasis on placement. Strategic holes have at least one reasonably safe navigation path to the hole, but it is usually the longest route. Any other route will be defended by hazards and obstacles. Driver is seldom the correct choice off the tee on strategic holes because the penalty for errant shots will be costly. Positioning is critical on strategic holes.

Penal holes typically give you just one option: either you can hit the shot or you pay the price. The par-3 17th hole at TPC Sawgrass is a classic penal hole. Although only 137 yards long, the tee shot is to an island green that is surrounded by water. The shot is "do or die." Execution and commitment are the keys on penal holes.

Heroic holes give you options. The 18th hole at Pebble Beach is an example of a classic heroic hole. The safe approach is to hit out to the right and then lay up short of the green. The heroic shot is to cut the corner and carry the ocean, giving you a chance to hit the green in two.

Shots Can Be Strategic, Penal, or Heroic Too

Sometimes a hole may start out as one type, but then change based on your circumstances. In that case even an individual shot can be thought of as strategic, penal, or heroic.

For example, a long par-4 may start out as heroic because if you crush a drive you'll have a short iron in to the green. But if your tee shot lands you in trouble, your next shot may suddenly be strategic if you can't reach the green, or even penal if your best option is to hit a wedge back to the fairway.

Short, Medium, and Long Holes

It may also be helpful to categorize holes as short, medium, or long. Be aware that short holes are often strategic and nearly always employ more robust defensive elements: narrow fairways, heavy bunkering or hazard complexes, or severely sloped greens. Identifying the defenses will tell you the best strategy to use.

Medium length holes will be less severely defended, often with only one significant defensive feature. Look for that one main defensive element on medium length holes. If you can get past it or around it you should find the hole receptive.

On long holes the natural defense is distance. Expect more options off the tee, as well as more ways to get the ball on the green besides an aerial attack. Look for runways, funnels, or mounds that facilitate running the ball into the green.

Understanding Green Complexes

Don't just look at the green. Look at all the features surrounding the green. Bunkers, trees, water, swales, mounds, and rough all serve a purpose. Together they make up what is referred to as the green complex. The more you pay attention to the entire green as a complex the more you will begin to decipher the architect's intentions and the message they are sending.

There are three distinctive green types: flat, concave, and convex.

Flat greens are easy, so expect them to be protected by a more hazardous complex surrounding them.

Concave greens will feed balls toward the middle, and would be considered "friendly" greens because they are receptive to approach shots. They will typically give you multiple options to attack the green. Look for the openings and the ways you could potentially work the ball off the higher surrounding ground to get your ball close to the hole.

Convex greens on the other hand, like those often found on Donald Ross courses, feed balls away from the green. They would be considered "unfriendly" greens and require thought about not only where you want to hit your ball, but also where you don't want to miss. Convex greens require precision in the approach shot.

Tiered greens can be any combination of flat, concave, and convex. The best way to understand tiered greens is to think about each tier as a mini-green. When you know which tier the pin is on, the rest of the green simply becomes part of the complex you need to analyze and either use to your advantage or guard against.

Beware of Illusions

Sometimes a hole's defense doesn't even look like a defense. Often the natural elements of the terrain create optical illusions that confound your sense of distance and cause mis-clubbing or uncertainty in the shot and lack of commitment. Features such as hills, swales, mounds, trees, and the raised lip of bunkers can hide the terrain between the feature and the pin. When the terrain is hidden our eyes trick us into thinking the terrain doesn't exist, making the pin seem closer than it actually is.

That's because our brains process depth perception using relative size (comparing similar objects in the near ground and fore ground), and familiarity (things we are already familiar with).

For example, since objects that are closer to us appear larger, a hole that has shorter trees in the foreground and larger trees farther away creates the illusion that the target is closer than it actually is. The opposite is true when trees in the near ground are tall and trees in the distance are smaller: the target will seem farther away.

Similarly a bunker with a prominent lip will draw the eye's attention. When the front portion of the bunker is made more prominent, or for that matter when the front portion of any hazard is made prominent, it will seem closer, creating the potential to underestimate the distance. When the back lip of a bunker or other hazard is made prominent the tendency is to overestimate the distance. It is important to pay attention to both the *near edge* and the *far edge* of bunkers and other hazards in order to judge distance correctly.

Every golf course has a mix of short, medium, and long holes that are also a mix of strategic, penal, and heroic holes. It is our job during playing lessons to help students understand what they are looking at *before* they reach for a club.

We often observe students seeing the hole in a new light when they start thinking in terms of strengths and weaknesses, attack vs. defense. Even on golf courses they play frequently!

•

Now that you understand design elements from an architect's perspective, let's take a look at our example hole. The par-5 we have been using for our case study has a number of strengths and weaknesses we need to consider before coming up with a strategy.

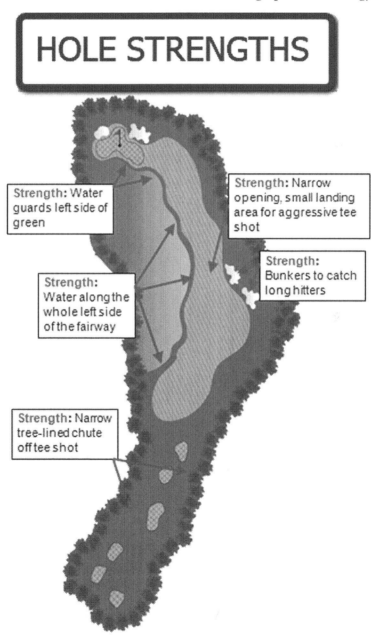

HOLE STRENGTHS

Strength: Water guards left side of green

Strength: Narrow opening, small landing area for aggressive tee shot

Strength: Water along the whole left side of the fairway

Strength: Bunkers to catch long hitters

Strength: Narrow tree-lined chute off tee shot

The water all along the left side is an obvious strength of the hole. Everybody gets that immediately. Because it is so large it dominates our perspective of the hole.

But we want our students to see much more than just the water, and it starts right from the tee box. Let's take a closer look at how we might identify strengths on this hole.

The architect designed this hole with a fairly narrow, tree-lined chute off the tee. That's the first "strength" of the hole because it requires a reasonably straight ball flight off the tee. A big curving hook or big slice with a driver won't work on this tee. The architect is saying "You'd better pick a club that doesn't curve much and a shot you don't push or pull."

The next thing we see from the tee box is the water on the left and the bunkers on the right side of the fairway.

It is much more penalizing to hit a ball into the water on the left, so the diabolical architect — knowing golfers will instinctively play away from the water — placed a bunker complex in a strategic position to catch golfers who hit driver, but bail out right.

Lastly we see that the fairway gets pinched in by the fairway bunker complex and the water the farther up the fairway you go. The small fairway landing area for the really long hitters is a strength of the hole. Essentially the architect is saying "If you are a long hitter AND you hit it straight I'm still going to make it challenging for you with a small landing area and trouble on both sides. But if you can pull it off I'll reward you with a shorter iron shot into the green and a chance for eagle."

Now let's look at weaknesses or soft-spots of the hole.

HOLE WEAKNESSES

Soft Spot: Wide landing area for approach shot. Plenty of bail out room.

Soft Spot: Flat putting surface in middle of green

Soft Spot: Wide fairway landing area. Lots of room to bail out right

From the tee we can see that the fairway in front of the bunkers is nice and wide. The wide fairway is a "soft spot" for the hole.

Most golfers will be able to get their ball comfortably into this area of the fairway, even when playing away from the water. The trade-off, of course, is that it will require laying up with a club other than the driver off the tee to stay short of the bunkers.

Laying up in front of the bunkers makes this a 3-shot hole to get home, so the architect is forcing you to make a decision right from the get-go on the tee.

Looking further up the fairway near the green we see another widening of the fairway in "scoring wedge" territory: from 70 to 125 yards. This wider section of fairway is another soft spot because it is a straightforward shot to get the ball safely in the right position to have a good angle at the pin, even if the golfer lays up on their tee shot in front of the bunkers.

We also see that the middle of the green is relatively flat: another soft spot, particularly when the pin is in the middle. By the same token, given the severity of the slope on the rest of this tiered green, any pin placements other than the middle of the green would require the precision of a scoring wedge shot to ensure the ball ends up in the correct tier and the correct quadrant below the hole.

Let's take a look at the entire hole from a strengths and weaknesses perspective.

Putting it all Together: Hole Strengths and Weaknesses

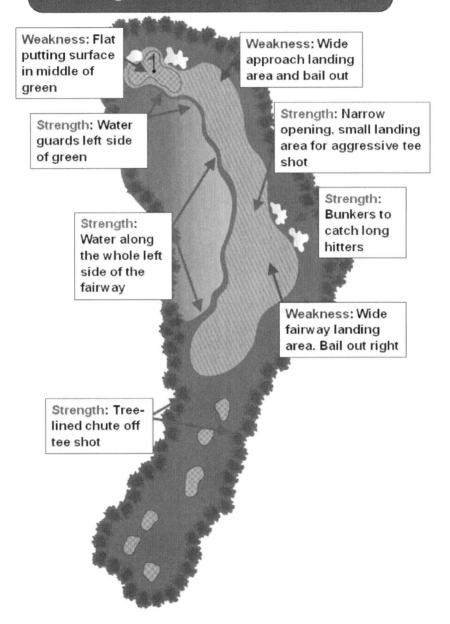

Weakness: Flat putting surface in middle of green

Weakness: Wide approach landing area and bail out

Strength: Water guards left side of green

Strength: Narrow opening, small landing area for aggressive tee shot

Strength: Water along the whole left side of the fairway

Strength: Bunkers to catch long hitters

Weakness: Wide fairway landing area. Bail out right

Strength: Tree-lined chute off tee shot

In summary our analysis shows us that the many strengths and hazards makes this a very difficult hole, particularly for the golfer who chooses to take an aggressive line. There are numerous defensive elements and ways for golfers to find trouble.

On the other hand the architect "softened" the hole considerably for golfers who elect to take the safe navigation route and play for the green in three shots. In many ways this is an "easy" par-5 for golfers who elect to get home in three because there are wide fairway layup areas and it is not a particularly long par-5.

It should be clear after this analysis that this particular hole would be classified as heroic.

Do You Have That Shot?

Remember from the beginning of the book that the three strategic golf questions you ask are:

- What does the shot require?
- Do I have that shot?
- Can I commit?

Your analysis of the hole will tell you what type of shot is required. The next step is to ask yourself whether you have the shot that fits the requirements.

We advise our students to compare the strengths and weaknesses of the hole to the strengths and weaknesses of their game (which we define as ball-striking ability) to judge their ability to pull off the shot.

Every golfer has strengths and weaknesses: things they do well and things they do not do well. The way the potential shots have been described to play this hole involves a number of different options as well as a number of possible different shot types. These shots could be played with full swings, 3/4-shots, knock-downs, or a host of other optional shot types.

If you don't have all these shots in your arsenal and could use a little help developing your skills I put together a wonderful training program called Brown Bag Golf at www.EricJonesGolf.com.

Brown Bag Golf is a series of weekly practice session lessons purposely structured so you can accomplish them in a short amount of time, like over your lunch hour. That's actually where the name came from: bring your lunch (which in the old days meant inside a brown paper bag) and get in a practice session while you eat, in less than an hour.

What makes Brown Bag Golf unique is that all the lesson sessions are performance-related rather than technique-related. They are designed to help you develop skills, rather than fix flaws. Fixing flaws is how you get your game back to normal. Developing skills is how you make your golf game better.

If we use putting as an example, the lessons don't necessarily tell you *how* to putt. They just show you how to *make* more putts.

Here's how Brown Bag Golf works …

We ask golfers all the time to list what they consider the most important shots in golf. The one that nearly always comes up first is the 6-foot putt. These are round-makers or round-breakers.

We know the Tour pros make this put more than 70% of the time. That's from all slopes and all breaks, as well as in tournament conditions. The average amateur, on the other hand, makes less than 33% of their 6-foot putts.

The measurement of how many putts you make is a performance statistic. Performance statistics don't measure technique. They only measure how many times the ball goes in the hole.

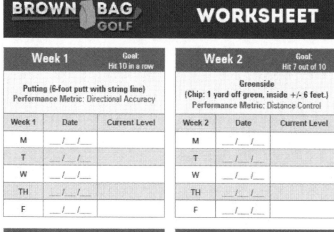

The Brown Bag Golf lesson on 6-foot putts, for example, shows you how to measure your stats from six feet. Then it shows you how to train yourself to make more putts.

In the lesson I show you how to set up a simple string line or chalk line, and how to start collecting your stats.

The lesson also describes the key variables that influence your stats like face angle at impact, club path, and stroke length. It shows you how to use the string line and a few tees for both analysis and training. Then the lesson shows you how to practice and train to improve your stats on this shot.

Brown Bag Golf covers all the most important shots in golf: Putting, Driving, Greenside, Scoring Wedges, and approach shots and fairway irons and woods. Click on the link to learn about and enroll in Brown Bag Golf.

Knowing your performance stats for all your clubs and all your shots is a key component in making good course navigation strategy decisions, because your stats tell you your strengths and weaknesses. This brings us to Course Navigation Principle #4: Play to the Strengths of Your Game.

•

COURSE NAVIGATION PRINCIPLE #4
PLAY TO THE WEAKNESS OF THE HOLE AND THE STRONG SUIT OF YOUR GAME

Your goal is to stack the odds in your favor by making intelligent strategic decisions that play to the strengths of your game and the weaknesses of the hole. The rule is simple: play to your strengths.

Knowing how the architect designed the hole to have strengths and weaknesses and how the hole is set up to defend against your attack is the first step to making good strategic decisions. Look for the weaknesses of the hole. Watch out for the strengths.

Never make a shot from a position of your own weakness where you are hitting into the teeth of the hole's strength. Instead, plan your next shot so that it puts you back in an area of your strength. Be willing to take your lumps.

Is Driver Your Strength, or Weakness?

Your number one objective off the tee should be to keep the ball in play, because the drive off the tee sets up the entire hole.

Is your driver a strength or weakness?

I had a long conversation about the importance of driving with a 26-year veteran of the LPGA tour and winner of the Women's U.S.

Open. She considered her driver to be a "scoring" club, because it set up the entire hole. With a good drive she could be aggressive on her next shot. With a poor drive she was forced to opt for the conservative approach. It's hard to score well when you are always on the defensive.

She worked very hard to turn her driver into a strength of her game, training for both distance and consistency.

But the average weekend warrior doesn't have the luxury of time to practice and train like the Pros. Which means that driver is probably not a strength of their game. Driver is one of the hardest clubs in the bag to hit with consistency.

Which means that when the tee shot is a strength from the hole's perspective the golfer would likely be better off leaving their driver in the bag. Instead, pick a navigation strategy and club that will get the ball in play. (If you want to hit your drives better I have a few driver training videos you can watch at EricJonesGolf.com.)

Be patient and wait for the opportunities to match your strength against the hole's weaknesses. You may find it an interesting exercise the next time you play to look at each hole and try to implement a "shot ranking" formula to compare the hole's strengths to your shot strengths. Assign a value between 1 and 10 to the defensive feature of the hole. Then assign a similar strength value to your ability to hit that shot with that club. When the hole's strength is bigger than your shot strength, find another strategy. When your shot strength is bigger than the feature strength, you have a green light.

Keeping the Ball in Play

Do your shots have a consistent shape, particularly with your driver? They should.

Hitting the ball straight — particularly off the tee — is one of the hardest shots in golf. Nearly every Tour Pro and well-known PGA teaching professional will advise you to shape your shots rather than try to hit them straight.

Pick a shape and master it.

Here's an interesting way to think about it: If you aim your drive up the middle of the fairway planning for a straight shot — and miss — you only have half the fairway (usually less than 15 yards) of wiggle room to either side.

The most common shot shape for amateurs — and the most prevalent shot shape on the PGA Tour — is a fade. If you aim up the left side of the fairway and play a fade but miss and hit a slice (the typical miss for a golfer who fades the ball), you have the entire width of the fairway for wiggle room. Even if you miss it straight you still end up on the left side of the fairway.

Shape your shots. As long as the shape is consistent, purposefully having a shape to your shots will give you a wider margin for error.

There's always a good place to hit a bad shot.

For course navigation purposes you also need to pick a target that will allow for your normal shot shape as well as your miss.

You're not going to hit every shot perfectly, so another benefit of understanding strengths and weaknesses is learning where to "not miss" a shot and where you can "bail out." In other words, you need to know where you can miss your shot.

EXAMPLE #1: The most common navigation strategy mistake is picking a target that could result in you "short-siding" yourself around the green.

Below we have an example of a pin tucked in the back right corner.

If you are a natural fader of the ball, or if your typical miss is to the right, you should never aim directly at a pin on the right. Your miss could get you in a lot of trouble because you'll short-side yourself either in a bunker or with an awkward lie and very little green to work with. The odds of recovery from a short-side miss are low.

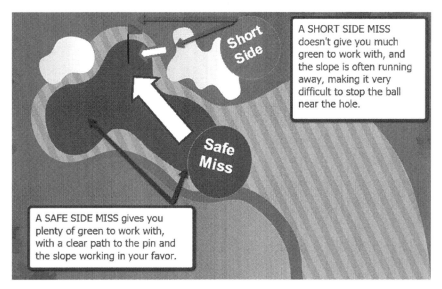

A SHORT SIDE MISS doesn't give you much green to work with, and the slope is often running away, making it very difficult to stop the ball near the hole.

A SAFE SIDE MISS gives you plenty of green to work with, with a clear path to the pin and the slope working in your favor.

The back right pin position is a strength of the hole because it is on a small shelf and is surrounded by bunkers. Normally it would be a difficult pin to reach. If you go right at the pin you are matching your weakness (a tendency to miss to the right) against the hole's strength.

But there is a way to turn this into a case of strength vs. strength.

If your strength is that you consistently fade the ball then the way you stack the odds in your favor is by picking the right navigation spot to aim at — in this case the middle of the green.

If you happen to hit it straight while aiming at the middle of the green you'd have an uphill putt from a safe position. If you aim at the middle and fade the ball or miss right, you could end up next to the hole — a happy miss.

Even if you don't make perfect contact and come up short, by picking a navigation target in the middle of the green your miss will wind up in the front of the green. That still gives you a straight path to the pin, avoids hazards, and allows you to use the slope to your advantage to make the next shot easier.

The key navigation consideration is to pick the right target to aim at. Play your normal shot shape and allow for your miss.

Let's take a look at another example off the tee.

EXAMPLE #2: If you can consistently shape your shots off the tee you will have an advantage because you will be able to hit more fairways and keep the ball in play more often than your competitors.

If your normal shot shape off the tee is a fade, then your navigation strategy for most holes will be similar: aim up the left side of the fairway and allow your fade to bring the ball back to the middle.

In the example below we have a dogleg left. There are trees and fairway bunkers guarding the left corner. There is also a bail-out area to the right side of the fairway that is wide enough to allow for your miss should you slice the ball (the typical miss for golfers who fade the ball).

In this case the hazards on the left work to your advantage because the corner of the first bunker will actually help you pick a specific target. The corner gives you a specific target to aim at.

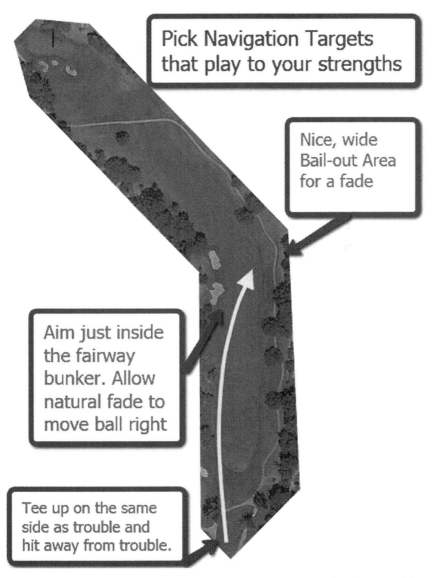

Pick a navigation line — your target — just inside the bunkers and let your natural shot take care of the rest. (Note: I never recommend aiming at a hazard you can reach. You can use it for aiming purposes, but aim just to the side of it).

There are a couple more guidelines you can follow to help stack the odds in your favor.

TEE POSITION: First, the tee box gives you some latitude about where you can tee up your ball to give you different angles to the fairway and the position you'd like to be in for your next shot. Take advantage of your ability to put the ball on one side or the other when on the tee box.

As a general rule, *tee up on the same side as trouble and hit away from trouble.* This will maximize the fairway area where you can position your shot.

Second, be aware that not all tee boxes and tee markers will be aligned to the direction or target you want to hit. In fact, architects will often design tee boxes to *purposely* aim you in the wrong direction.

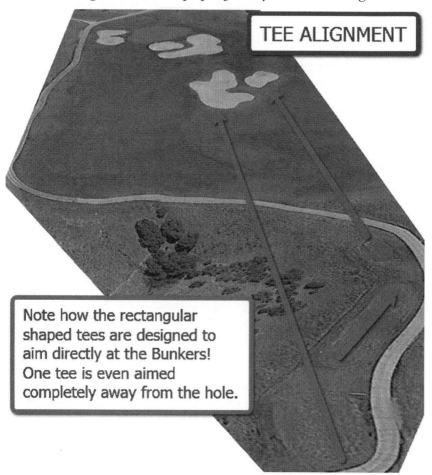

TEE ALIGNMENT

Note how the rectangular shaped tees are designed to aim directly at the Bunkers! One tee is even aimed completely away from the hole.

It is very difficult to ignore the lines of the tee box or the orientation of the tee blocks on the grass. That's because we use them subconsciously to help us with alignment. Tee markers placed by the grounds crew are more often located in positions to help save grass than they are to help with your alignment.

DON'T automatically tee up your golf ball directly between the tee blocks. They may not be aimed where you want to go!

We had a lot of fun with this one during a playing lesson (see image).

The course has a par-3 where the rectangular teeing surface is aimed 50 yards to the right of the hole — directly at a restroom. As my student took his stance and I quietly pointed out to the other two students where he was aimed.

The student, Charles, hit a great shot. The only problem was that it flew directly to his target — the restroom.

When I pointed out how the tee box was designed to aim him to the right, he claimed that he had not used the tee box for alignment.

So we had Charles hit another ball.

Sure enough he did exactly the same thing: he teed his ball up right between the tee blocks, aimed straight at the restroom, and hit it in the exact same place.

After we finished laughing he swore that the tee box lines weren't influencing his alignment.

So we had him hit a third shot.

Only this time we put a couple of clubs down on the ground and aimed them directly at the pin. We put the ball between the alignment clubs just to be absolutely sure he was aiming at the right target.

When Charles lined up for his third shot, using the alignment clubs, he lined up perfectly. Then he proceeded to hit a slice — right back to the restroom.

The point is to be aware of the subtle influences that could affect your shot, even at the subconscious level. When the shot doesn't feel like it lines up correctly for you, or if it doesn't "suit your eye" as the Pros say, you need to pay special attention to your target, and find a way to exclude everything else.

PS: That rest room has forever after been referred to by students as the "Chuck Stop", named after Charles and the famous lesson he helped us all learn about tee box lines and alignment.

Which brings us to the next Principle #5: Pick Specific Targets.

•

COURSE NAVIGATION PRINCIPLE #5
HIT TO SPECIFIC TARGETS

Once you have determined your strategy for playing the hole and for playing each shot, the last crucial piece of execution is to pick specific targets and hit to those targets.

I can't overemphasize the importance of picking specific targets.

Specific Instructions Lead to Specific Results

Your body performs best when it is trying to achieve a specific objective. We'll discuss why in the third companion book to this series *"Play Strategic Golf: Mental Toughness"*. But the idea is that the more specific your brain's instructions are to the body, the more likely you will get the result you want.

There is a golf saying that advises "Aim small to miss small." If you follow that advice it will improve your accuracy.

If your goal is just to "hit the fairway" you have only a general goal. "Fairway" is too broad a target, and the instructions are not specific enough for your body to interpret accurately. Somewhere in the middle of your swing your body will be wondering exactly which part of the fairway you meant. You'll wind up with an indecisive swing that probably won't get you the results you want.

The Smaller the Target the Better

Once you have a specific navigation strategy for the hole, pick a specific target for each shot where you would like your shot to end up. The smaller the target the better. Pick a marker, a distinct shade of grass, or at the very least a landmark on the horizon. Get totally focused on that target and nothing else. Then let your club release to that target.

From a course navigation standpoint this means you have to take the time to identify a specific target before each shot.

Not a direction. Not a side of the fairway or green. Not an area.

A *very* specific target.

There is a well-known story about Ben Hogan who asked his caddy for advice on where to hit his drive on a blind tee shot. When the caddy told him to aim for the trees on the left, Hogan's response was "Which tree?"

That's how specific you should be on all your shots.

Don't just navigate. Navigate to specific spots.

TARGET AIMING POINTS

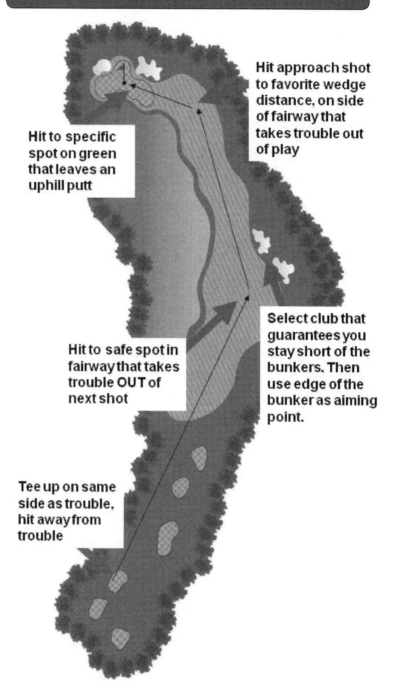

Hit approach shot to favorite wedge distance, on side of fairway that takes trouble out of play

Hit to specific spot on green that leaves an uphill putt

Hit to safe spot in fairway that takes trouble OUT of next shot

Select club that guarantees you stay short of the bunkers. Then use edge of the bunker as aiming point.

Tee up on same side as trouble, hit away from trouble

Using Lines to Pick Targets

There is another course navigation strategy employed by many PGA Tour pros involving "lines" that helps with consistency and positioning as well as picking out specific targets. It involves imagining a line from your ball to the target and then either crossing or not crossing the line.

For example, Jack Nicklaus used to imagine a line up the fairway for his tee shots. When he played he disciplined himself to "not cross the line" with any of his shots. He knew that by using this strategy he effectively took one side of the golf course out of consideration, and kept himself on the "safe" side of the green on approach shots.

The second example involves imagining two lines. The two lines define a corridor or a landing area where you want your shot to end up (usually your drive or par-5 second shot). With two lines you want to make sure you cross the first one, but stay short of the second one. The lines will help you identify a specific target.

Let's take a specific example of using two lines on a short par-4. This example is from *"How To Make A Yardage Book"* using a Google Earth image with a centerline drawn from the tee to the green.

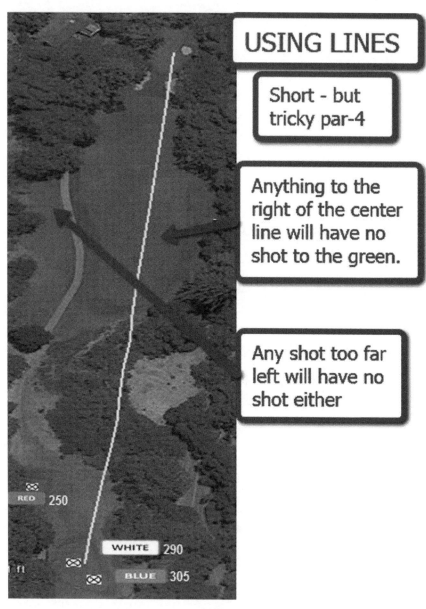

USING LINES

Short - but tricky par-4

Anything to the right of the center line will have no shot to the green.

Any shot too far left will have no shot either

RED 250

WHITE 290

BLUE 305

In this example we have a short, 305-yard par-4. It's tricky because there are trees that guard the entrance to the green on both sides. The only way to reach the green is through a narrow opening, which means there is only a narrow area on the fairway that permits a straight shot into the green.

In the first image we see the entire hole, with a centerline drawn from the tee to the green. This would be an example of using a single line. You want to keep your ball to the left of the line, because anything to the right of the line will result in a second shot blocked by the trees guarding the green.

But since there are trees on the left side of the green guarding that side as well, this is a good hole to make use of two lines.

In the second image we see the same hole, zoomed in to the landing area in front of the green. We've drawn a second line using the trees on the left side of the green to establish the left side angle. The result is a corridor where we'd like the ball to finish, because anything within the corridor will have a straight shot at the pin.

USING LINES

Close-up of the landing area

Because the angles into the green are protected by trees and are so narrow, the actual target landing area is a corridor on the fairway. You must cross the line on the right, but not cross the line on the left.

We've also marked down some yardages to specific spots that help make club selection easier. The 220/70 means a 220-yard tee shot, leaving 70 yards to the middle of the green. The 190/100 is a 190-yard tee shot that would leave a 100-yard approach shot. Then we put a big "GO" sign in the middle of the corridor as a reminder of our target. This example of hitting to a corridor, by the way, is taken from my *"How To Make A Yardage Book"* instruction manual. Even if you never make a yardage book it is worth reading to help you understand how you should be looking at the hole to pick angles and landing spots.

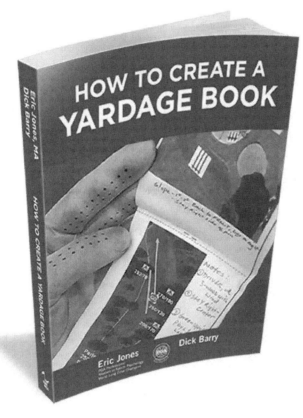

COURSE NAVIGATION PRINCIPLE #6
PLAN A STRATEGY IN ADVANCE
FOR THE TOUGHEST HOLES

Lastly, almost every golf course will have one or two really tough holes. They may be tough for everybody, or just particularly tough for you. You can find them on the scorecard because they will often be ranked as the #1 and #2 handicap holes.

The point of this rule of thumb is to not let the tough holes beat you.

My advice to you would be to take the time to create a navigation strategy for all 18 holes. But if that's not a practical option for you, I'd like to give you an alternative that will save you strokes.

Have a plan for the one or two toughest holes on the course.

My uncle, Tom Seaver, was a professional baseball pitcher for the Mets. His description of how he would prepare for games is relevant to the way you should prepare for the course you will be playing.

Tom spent most of his mental preparation time thinking about how he would pitch to the one or two toughest hitters in the line-up. He would imagine all the various scenarios where he might face these tough hitters. Then he would imagine what he would do to handle those situations.

His goal (and yours on the course) was straightforward: he did not want to let the best hitters in the line-up beat him. By thinking ahead of all the different scenarios under which he would be facing these tough hitters, and how he would pitch in those situations, he didn't have to devise a strategy on the fly. When the situation came up, he already knew what he would do. It's this kind of thinking that led to his induction into the Baseball Hall of Fame.

Take the advice of one of the best players in the game: Don't let the one or two toughest holes on the course beat you. Devise a strategy in advance to handle them.

Make a strategy. Find the weakest points of the hole, and match your strongest points against the hole's weak points. At the very least, plan a strategy to take advantage of your strengths on the tough holes.

The First Drive of the Day

Sometimes the hardest shot you'll hit is the first drive of the day. Do you have first-tee jitters? Does it take a few holes before your game settles down and you start playing your regular game?

A few years ago I worked with a young, aspiring Tour pro. He was a great player, but it always took him the first couple of holes to get in the groove. He couldn't afford to start the round with bogeys or worse. He wanted to find a way to come right out of the gate playing his best golf.

To help him I wrote down a series of specific steps to take before each round — everything I had learned as a competitor myself and from my studies in Sport Psychology relevant to getting off to a fast start. We refined the steps and skills until we developed a complete warm-up/prep routine that took him 55 minutes before the start of the tournament. It worked like a charm. Later I shared the steps with several ladies groups who wanted to know how to handle first tee jitters. It worked for them as well.

I started giving seminars on how to handle first-tee jitters. The seminars led me to write everything down and put it in a program, which I wound up calling the *"A-Game Cheat Sheet."* It's a video, and audio podcast, and a written explanation of the steps you can take to bring your best game to the course and the first tee every time you play. Click the A-Game Cheat Sheet link to learn more.

Here are the major prep-steps in the A-Game Cheat Sheet:

1. Slow down to Golf Time;
2. Putt first (which putts, how, how many);
3. Warm up correctly (what clubs to hit and how);
4. Figure out what shot you have that day (no fixing the swing);
5. Hit strategic shots (approach shots, par-3s, toughest hole);
6. End with the shot you will hit on the 1st tee.

•

SUMMARY

Let's sum up Course Navigation.

Framework

Three buckets form the Play Strategic Golf framework, and the framework will help you create your strategy as well as help you analyze your performance.

1. Course Navigation
2. Game Management
3. Self Management

Course Navigation

Course "management" is easier to understand by thinking in terms of course "navigation." Successful Course Navigation means positioning yourself on the course, shot by shot, to have the easiest path to your target and the easiest shot.

There are six Course Navigation Principles to help you develop your shot strategy:

1. Plan your current shot to make your next shot as easy as possible.
2. Plan your strategy for each hole from the cup back to the tee.
3. Attack only easy pins.
4. Play to the weakness of the hole and the strong suit of your game.
5. Hit to specific targets.
6. Plan a course strategy, or at least have a strategy in advance for the toughest holes.

•

I hope you have enjoyed book 1 of the "Play Strategic Golf" series.

Eric Jones
Northern California PGA 2014 Teacher of the Year
Masters in Sport Psychology
2-time World Long Drive Champion
####

FREE STUFF

Thank you for picking up **Play Strategic Golf: Course Navigation**. It is my sincerest hope that inside these pages you will find information that will help you play better golf and have more fun on the course. Helping people is why I became a teaching professional, and whether it is through books, videos, or on the lesson tee, my greatest reward is when students experience that "Aha!" moment that changes everything for them.

But like you, I am also a learner. I never stop reading and researching and experimenting to find new and better ways to break through to the next performance level. So as you read this book and find typos, areas that are confusing, ideas that you think could use some expansion or more examples, or anything else that comes to mind, please send me an email with your thoughts. If there is any way you think this book could be improved, I'd love to have you send your comments to me at books@ericjonesgolf.com

I have a **free mini-report** available for you as another way to thank you for picking up this book. It's called *"Playing Yardage: The Secret to Scoring."* It's a primer I put together to help my students with their approach shots — in particular their scoring wedge shots from 70-125 yards. It will help you get your ball closer to the pin more consistently. Just visit ericjonesgolf.com/resources and enter your name and email so I can send you the primer.

PS: I produce about a book a year. If you'd like to join the early-bird notification list for future book releases, please click to sign up for my email Notification List on my site at www.EricJonesGolf.com. I also give golfers on this list first crack at signing up to be Alpha Readers and my crowdsourcing collaborators, where you can offer comments and suggestions on pre-release book drafts and be a part of the final version.

•

ERIC JONES

ABOUT THE AUTHOR

ERIC JONES is a PGA Class "A" teaching professional and a two-time winner of the World Long Drive Championship. A former player and Assistant Coach at Stanford University, he is one of the few PGA professionals holding a Master's degree in Sport Psychology. His innovative approach to instruction and coaching led to him being named the 2014 PGA Teacher of the Year in Northern California.

An accomplished competitor, Eric won the World Long Drive Champion Senior title in 2003, and the Super-Senior title in 2012. Along the way he captured the 2004 Rookie of the Year honors on the LDA Long Drive Tour, and in 2006 became the only long driver to simultaneously win both the Senior and Open division titles at the Players Tour Long Drive Championship.

As the founder of the Eric Jones Golf Academy, his Golf Coach Program has received national attention for its unique approach to teaching the whole game, not just swing mechanics, and for its effectiveness with students of all levels. The Academy conducts programs for both juniors and adults year-round.

Eric is the author of multiple game improvement golf books, including: *"The 5 Keys To Distance"*, *"The Practice Effect"*, *"Radar For Golf"*, and the *"Strategic Golf"* series. He has also developed numerous online training programs which are available at ericjonesgolf.com/resources. He has published more than 100 articles on golf and is a contributor to the popular "A Lesson Learned" for the PGA of America. Eric is a frequent keynote speaker at trade and industry events, including the Northern California Golf Expo. He is a member of the Flightscope Academy teaching faculty and serves on the board of advisors for several golf-related companies, including Game Golf.

Eric is passionate about helping all people learn and enjoy their golf game and he brings a unique perspective to his craft. As a world class athlete he understands what it takes to compete and excel at the highest levels and he revels in using his experience to help students reach their own highest level of performance regardless of their age or skill level.

You can reach Eric at books@ericjonesgolf.com, subscribe to his future book releases at Book Notifications, and view his Kindle Author page.

•

THE CROWDSOURCE COLLABORATION TEAM

One of the most interesting aspects of writing this book was the final editing process. This book is dedicated to them.

Rather than go the traditional route of hiring a professional editor I decided to experiment with crowdsourcing. My thinking was that the combined wisdom of many golfers would create a final version that would be far better than what any one of us could produce individually.

Crowdsourcing involves inviting many people to contribute to a project. It is a relatively new phenomenon made possible by advances in online technology that combine multi-user access with file sharing and version control. We did it using Google Drive and Google docs.

It was a fascinating experience.

Since this was my first attempt at crowdsourcing, I didn't quite know what to expect. I sent an invitation out to students and golfers who had purchased one of my training programs. My hope was to entice perhaps a couple of dozen golfers to take the time out of their already busy schedule to not only read the initial draft, but to scrutinize it, think about the content, and offer their opinions.

I was worried that it might be a bit much to ask, and as I hit the send button it was with one of those "What if I throw a party and nobody comes?" feelings.

But I shouldn't have worried. Golfers are an amazing bunch. Maybe it's because no matter where we are we all share the same experience. We go into battle. We come out the other side. Along the way our triumphs and disasters create the stories that make up the warp and woof of the game we love. It's why we play, and it's that shared fabric of experience that makes golfers want to help other golfers.

I was hoping for a couple of dozen collaborators. Fifty would have been great. So it was absolutely amazing to see that within hours *several hundred* golfers signed up to collaborate. Not only was it a party, it was rip-roaring. And they all had something to say.

Fair warning though: crowdsourcing the final edits of a book is not for the faint of heart. Many sections I thought were good had to be torn apart and rebuilt. It can be a humbling experience. Plus there were thousands of comments. Time consuming as it was, I read and responded to every one. I owed them that.

In the end I found crowdsourcing to be an insightful, interesting, challenging, and ultimately rewarding experience. There is no doubt the book is better because of the insights of the contributors. I am a better writer because of their feedback.

You can understand, then, why I am deeply grateful to those golfers who volunteered to collaborate. I hope you got as much out of the process as I did.

Here are the golfers who took the time to crowdsource and collaborate with me to produce the final version of this book:

Maureen McInaney-Jones, Dick Barry, Leith Anderson, Lisa Cobler, Dave Adams, Glen Albaugh, John Allen, Bosse Backman, David Bagshaw, Brent Barker, Jesse Barker, Bobby Barley, Norman Bartlett, Gary Bays, Janie Bell-Westcott, Scott Benson, John Bentley, Tom Bernthal, Sunil Bhalla, Stefano Bignozzi, Harvey Bishop, Milton Black, Richard Blayden, Alejandro Bonbonso, Marc Bourget, Robert Bright, Gary Brown, Luis Buxo, Bev Cabellon, Doug Cakebread, Michael Calev, Alan Campbell, Andy Chalot, Steve Chapman, Raymond Chastel, Brian Cloke, Dave Collett, Donald Corby, John Corley, Fernando Cortes, Edward Costello, Jerry Crank, Jim Crawford, Jeffrey Curran, Tim Darr, David Davies, Alan Depew, Bob Dills, Don Dolenec, Ko Dooms, Bill Durrett, Bill Epter, Dave Everitt, Steve Falzone, Ron Farmer, Erik Farrar, John Feagler, John Fitzgerald, Donal Foran, John Forsyth, Ron Frank, Tony Freeburn, Shone Freeman, Tom Frey, Stuart Fulton, T.Parker Gallagher, Roger Gaw, Axel Gebauer, Jack Geiger, Chris Goble, Joseph Gonzalez, Rajesh Gopalakrishna, Jim Graham, Norm Graulich, Donald

Greenhow, Rick Greenough, Ron Greig, Ricardo Grenough, Tim Griesbach, Gary Gross, Mark Grottoli, Hlodver Gudnason, Alain Guillou, Kurt Harms, Clark Harrell, Colin Harris, Laurilee Hatcher, Jerry Hauck, Dan Haynosch, Joe Healey, George Hendey, Conrad Herwig, Chuck Hinners, Staffan Holmstedt, Larry Hunter-Blank, Jacob Hutt, Terry Jacobs, Larry Jaskolka, Chuck Jensen, Eric Jones, Reginald Jones, Juan Jose Reynoso, Sandor Juhasz, Sean Kelleher, Mike Kelly, Bill Kerney, Jim Kerr, Tony Key, Ryan Ki, William King, John Knight, Chris Knobloch, Rick Kriz, Jean-marie Laforge, Lawrence Lang, Edwin Lee, Yun Lei, Walter Leong, Orson Leong, Allan Levine, Chuck Lewandowski, Dean Libner, Dayin Lin, Daniel Lopez, Frank Luchsinger, Rick MacDonald, Greg Mainis, Paul Major, Ramesh Mallya, Randall Matheny, Matthew McCarthy, John McKinlay, Bren McLaughlin, John Menefee, Jr, Laurence Merchant, Wayne Miller, Arthur Minadeo, Don Mitchell, Daniel Monroe, Ray Montgomery, Andy Morris, David Morrison, Luke Mueller, Shan Mugavadivelu, Kevin Murphy, Jim Murphy, Roger Nicandro, Amauri Nunes, Mike O'Donnell, Hinrich Oltmann, John O'Neill, Howard Owens, Graham Parker, Allan Patrick, Paul Pazdan, Jorma Pekkanen, William Pennington, Hans Peter Furrer, Wolfgang Petereit, Pete Peterik, Stephen Petrie, Paul Petry, Sam Pochucha, Harold Pohoresky, Michael Politsch, Norval Prakash, Graham Presland, Andre Pretorius, Ivan Randall, David Reed, Axel Regeniter, Dominick Rencricca, Brian Rendine, Ivan Rhodes, Art Riben, Walter Rogers, Nadine Rosenzweig, David Rostad, John Ruark, George Rugys, Larry Salk, Rob Schuller, Shel Schumaker, Bob Sciutto, Felix Semion, Atulya Sharma, Larry Shaw, Jeff Shepherd, Gary Simpkins, Richard Singer, Surjeet Singh, Michael Singsen, Jim Sklencar, John Sohn, Pietro Soldini, Vivek Sood, Jane Southcombe, Brendan Spicer, Sean Starkey, Venkat Sundaram, Nollie Swynnerton, Shuh-Chern Tan, Warwick Thomas, Chris Thompson, Alex Thorne, Jim Toellner, Tex Toohey, Chuck Tyler, George Uber, Erik van de Pontseele, Peter Voss, Kevin Walsh, Carl Watson, Ted Way, Craig Wells, Pete Wick, Jon Williams, Terry Wilson, Doc Wilson, David Wiltse, Susan Winfree, Michael Winn, Zee Wong, Bryson Worley, Robert Worobec, Lance Wrobel, Grant Wyborny, Chuck Yaeger, Phil Young, Tony Zoppi.

•

RESOURCES

FREE STUFF

"*Playing Yardage: The Secret to Scoring*" by Eric Jones. A free downloadable guide to understanding how to calculate playing yardages and how to match the shot yardage to your club carry distances. A fantastic way to get your approach shots closer to the hole and great info.

FREE VIDEOS

Driver Training Videos: Fix These Speed Killers

Driver Training Videos: Get More Distance

Scoring Shots Training Videos

BOOKS

"*Play Strategic Golf: Game Management*" by Eric Jones. Published by Birdie Press. Available on Kindle

"*Play Strategic Golf: Mental Toughness*" by Eric Jones. Published by Birdie Press. Available on Kindle.

"*How To Practice Your Golf Swing Like The Pros*" by Eric Jones. Published by Birdie Press. Available on Kindle.

"*How To Make A Yardage Book*" by Eric Jones and Dick Barry. Published by Birdie Press. Available on Kindle.

"*Winning The Battle Within*" by Glen Albaugh. Published by Kele Publishing. Available directly from the author at www.wbwgolf.com. You can read my review of the book by visiting my site.

"*Flow in Sports*: The Keys to Optimal Experiences and Performances" by Susan Jackson and Mihaly Csikszentmihalyi. Published by Human Kinetics. Available at http://www.humankinetics.com/products/all-products/flow-in-sports. One of the best books I've ever read when it comes to understanding The Zone and peak athletic performance.

"*The Practice Effect*: How To Groove A Reliable, Automatic Golf Swing You Can Trust" by Eric Jones and John Snopkowski. Published by Birdie Press. Available on Kindle.

"*Radar For Golf*: The Future of Teaching, Training, and Clubfitting" by Eric Jones and Leith Anderson. Published by Birdie Press. Available on Kindle.

"*Lessons from the Golf Guru*: Wit, Wisdom, Mind Tricks, & Mysticism for Golf and Life" by Mike Dowd, PGA. A delightful and insightful book by one of my fellow PGA professionals. Written in a friendly and approachable style, the book is like dropping by Mike's office for a chat about things that really matter — in golf and in life. Available on Kindle.

TRAINING PROGRAMS

"*The 5 Keys To Distance*: How To Drive The Golf Ball Farther" by Eric Jones. Published by Birdie Press. This is the complete training program Eric uses each year to prepare for the World Long Drive Championships. This best-selling program is used by more than 10,000 golfers to hit longer, more consistent drives. Includes DVDs, hard-copy book "The 5 Keys To Distance", and an online training portal.

"*The Performance Coaching Program*" by Eric Jones. A monthly coaching program designed to improve your strategic and tactical skills on the golf course. Everything that has to do with playing golf, except anything that has to do with the golf swing.

"Brown Bag Golf" by Eric Jones. How to have a smart practice session in less than an hour. A weekly video-based training system of 26 practice sessions you can complete on your lunch hour.

"A-Game Cheat Sheet" by Eric Jones. How to bring your "A" game to the course every time. A series of steps and lessons with video, text, and podcasts that will get you prepared to play your best golf, every time.

"Scoring Clubs" by Eric Jones. How to dial in your distances for one of the most important shots in golf: your wedges from 70 to 125 yards. Includes instructions for full-swing and 3/4-swing. Program comes complete with video and online training portal.

####

This book is available in quantity at special discounts for your group or organization. For further information please contact:

Birdie Press
21 C Orinda Way #236
Orinda, CA 94563
www.birdiepress.com

Disclaimer and Limitation of Liability

Golf by its very nature contains some inherent risk of injury. The information presented in this book is for your reference and entertainment, and you, as the reader/end-user, are ultimately responsible for judging the suitability of the exercises and activities as they relate to your unique circumstances. Please use good judgment. This book is not intended as legal or physical advice. If you are in doubt, consult a physician or other competent professional. While attempts have been made to verify information provided in this publication, neither the author nor the publisher assumes any responsibility for any damages, including special, incidental, consequential, or other damages whatsoever, or for errors, omissions, or contradictory information contained herein. No representations or warranties are made or implied, including with respect to the accuracy or completeness of the contents of the book or for any claims for performance.

####

15924952R00050

Printed in Poland
by Amazon Fulfillment
Poland Sp. z o.o., Wrocław